Joshua I

5 Steps
TO
Self-fulfillment
Habits For A Balance Life

Dedication

With my deepest love, I dedicate this book to my late Grandparents Jesse & Eliza Penn may their values forever inspire me.

Table of Contents

Introduction

Creating this book gave me great pleasure, discovering what I would call "Life Hacks" and having the urge to share my findings. It is really me attempting to share the peace & happiness I've been granted in-spite of life's challenges, which we all face to some degree. My intention is to make it as easily understandable as possible, as well as, explain the power of the steps combined, in regards to positive change in ones life. I hope all who read this book practice these steps daily and create the quality of life they've always wanted; most of all, impart your newly found wisdom upon someone in need of tranquility. As I take you on my journey of self-elevation, it is important to note that I experienced the order in which the steps are illustrated as essential as the step themselves. Furthermore, exemplify that organized balance is the one true goal. Self-fulfillment is within everyone's grasp—those who wish to obtain it. Desire being the driving force in converting your dreams and wishes into tangible realities.

Step 1

MEDITATE

Reaching the understanding that the pathway to self-improvement is to take one day at a time. Creating daily habits to bring balance is essential for Self-fulfillment and Overall Health. Discovering the fore-mentioned, took some patience and deep thinking, arriving at the end of long days feeling like something was missing or the day was not as productive as it should have been or forgetting to do something important. It began to take a toll on my mental state which in turn started to effect my attitude. Sacrificing my time while continually overthinking on how to fill this void and deal with challenges of everyday life was frustrating to say the least. The origin of this book came out of a time where I felt my personal goals of self-improvement were being eclipsed by the need to complete monetary tasks. The stress and lack of balance became daunting. Being in a consistent state of stress whether physical, mental or emotional due to our busy agenda or anxiety for the future to come, can be suffocating and detrimental to the peace we seek. Regardless of age, stress for all generations is unhealthy and levels will increase as time goes on, if habits do not change. Increasing levels of cortisol "stress hormone" could impair learning and memory, lower immune function and bone density, also increasing blood pressure, cholesterol and chances of heart disease. There are a number of ways chronic stress could kill you. Luckily, there is a solution: meditation. By definition, meditation is thinking deeply or focusing one's mind for a period of time, in silence or with the aid of chanting, for religious or spiritual purposes or as a method of relaxation. The most effective forms, teach one to recognize thoughts that are harmful or may be self-defeating. The point is that as you gain understanding of your thought patterns, so that you can shift them toward more positive practices. It has been proven that meditating on a regular basis both clears the mind, allowing a true connection with the higher form of ones' self. It starts elevation by aiding in chakra alignment, also mitigating stress and anxiety, clear clogged pathways, decrease blood pressure and let more oxygen into the blood to reduce the strain on the heart. Starting each day with meditation is key to a clear, focused experience going forward on multiple health levels. When it comes to things that are important to me everyday, completing a 30 minute of daily meditation, is Step 1.

JOSHUA PENN, CNHP

Step 2

EXERCISE

Evaluating our mental state is the beginning stages of development, having a clear focus on where we currently are or a goal-oriented-mind allows a solid base to be made. Upon which all enhancements are possible and tangible results are within reach. *Along with the mental aspect to overcome there were physical activities that seemed not to be met, which also became a issue to accomplish for multiple reasons.* Some of which were feeling exhausted after work, mentally ran down, physically drained and less motivated as it became later in the day. I have since come to the realization that properly dividing your time is the key. Following the motto "Decide, Plan, Execute" is the foundation needed when your intentions on being successful at any task is a true desire. "Deciding" will turn out to be the most difficult but most important of all three. Indecision is a haltering practice that will prove to be self-evident as you continue your health journey and this book. One of the most health forming acts we can do is exercising, not only is it essential for proper body function it rivals mediation in its ability to eliminate stress & depression. Its aptitude to transform a sedentary body with the aide of consistency into a athletic healthy physique is breathtaking. The newly energized, well rested body will operate similar to a computer whose malware and viruses were removed. Strengthening the heart and lungs, clear veins and arteries, reducing blood sugar levels and controlling weight just to name a few, benefits gained through exercise. *However, clarity of mind is a attribute often overlooked when exercise is considered, outside of the external change the brain experience effects that would aide someone interested in improving theirselves on a holistic level.* Consistent exercise creates a healthy brain encouraging brain cell growth, which improves memory, as well as, protecting thinking skills. Boosting the cognitive abilities is necessary for developing self-awareness and accountability which are critical elements in fully understanding one's self to intelligently affect change. The happiness acquired from a more functional mind and body are priceless, raising us to levels never before achieved while aiding in a deeper discovery of what truly fulfills us. The fore-mentioned was hidden previously by a clouded mind & unhealthy body. Being active 30 minutes a day or 800 calories burned per workout session is the second step to a healthier life.

JOSHUA PENN, CNHP

Step 3

EAT CLEAN

Equally, if not more important to what we do with our bodies, is what we put in them. Education about nutrition and how it effects the mind, body & spirit are often ignored. Our speedy lifestyles in combination with the consistent barrage of creatively disguised junk foods contribute to lower, overall vitality. Observing the current state of weight gain in America, with many of Americans overweight and half of them obese, the necessity for a healthier way of eating is all but apparent. The three leading causes of death are heart disease, stroke & cancer which are directly associated with obesity, further illustrating the dangers of our present dietary choices. With our list of things-to-do continually increasing, along with seemingly less hours per day, the option for "fast food" appears as a perfect match; but nothing could be more misleading. The extra weight carried by most people is an obstruction to physical activity essential for feeling more vibrant as covered in Step 2. The lack of motivation due to chronic fatigue adversely encourages continuation of this debilitating cycle. Among preventable causes of disease obesity is a top the list, addiction to the very foods that cause these illnesses is a severe issue., not only for us interested in elevating to a higher level of consciousness, but to all who consume these types of food in this manner. Please note that this says, eat 'clean', emphasis on the clean. On my journey I found that changing my diet to a plant-based style was the cornerstone to my ascension. Removing toxic foods freed my body from struggling to eliminate them, bringing me to a healthier more balance state. With the new truly rested body I was able to feel good enough to see things in a relaxed positive light. Eating clean involves, taking the right amount of nutrition your body needs into your system, eating foods that give you the energy to power your spiritual voyage. Eating clean also involves a diet rich in vegetables, predominated by fruits, with nuts and seeds; a balanced diet of what we were designed to eat naturally, would bring us optimum health, it is for the sole purpose of applying those things learned. The most intriguing one for me is eating clean, gives us the vital energy to complete more health increasing acts, which brought a better overall quality of life and longevity, diet with a high glycemic load may cause increased symptoms of depression and fatigue. Conversely the longest living population on earth ate vegan-vegetarian diet of around mostly carbohydrates, low protein and fat with many foods eaten raw! My point here remains that, eating fresh whole foods whenever possible is a start to improving your mood, it can lighten up your life, and get you fueled for your fulfillment.

JOSHUA PENN, CNHP

Step 4

LEARN

Learning can be defined as gaining or acquiring knowledge. In simple terms, one is learning when one is becoming informed of something or finding something out. Especially when it benefits your true purpose. One should deliberately, consciously, and intentionally always want to learn. People perish due to the lack of knowledge. Most prominently knowledge of self. This obvious fundamental focus is at the core of self-fulfillment, wise to one's purpose through education of self is the road map to pure bliss that has been missing from your life. The whole of life, from the very moment you are born to the moment you die, is a process of learning. Acquiring information helps you to expand your horizon, and broaden your knowledge with the sole intent to pass the information on to make someone else better. You can also learn out of curiosity. It does not necessarily have to be an academic material, or something in your field. When you reach this understanding, that your information is not just important to you, but impacts others. It ignites your spirit, and it imparts affluence upon you. Know something about everything. However, you should apply selectivity and taste to whatever you are learning, although no knowledge is lost. Learning equips you to live in a world that feels almost impossible to live in. We can learn for different reasons, to acquire different skills, for recreational purposes, one learns naturally; learning cannot be undermined, and that is why learning can be done consciously and unconsciously. Sometimes, things we pick up from our immediate environment, school and places of work, forms a habit. Which is why obtaining beneficial habits only is ideal. Learning is no doubt a step to self-fulfillment because we are growing; you are developing your knowledge base and there is an increase in the value of your productivity, becoming better by the day, just from experience. When you recently discover something, you get an access to explore from a wide range of opportunities, and, to try new experiences. Learning also helps you to be in vogue, and to know the current happenings around you, hence, you can align with purpose, isn't that amazing?! The statement, 'learning is a core need for psychological wellbeing, and can help build confidence and self-efficacy', is true, because at the end of the day, whatever you have learned over the years, or that you have in your brain, is what helps you with 'life tests' whether it be good or bad. In order to be self-fulfilled, you must grow internally and spread the wealth. Learning one new thing each day is Step 4.

JOSHUA PENN, CNHP

Step 5

POSITIVITY

Law of attraction states that the belief that positive or negative thoughts bring positive or negative experiences into a person's life. Now, focusing on the positive, do you know how better your life would be, if you choose to focus on the positive alone? Most of us are clouded with so many negative thoughts, that hinder us from being self-fulfilled, questions like 'What if I fail?', 'What if this marriage doesn't work out?', 'I can't do it.' We are what we think we are, whether that is a failure or a success. Saying, "I can do it!', 'and watch how everything within you, responds and reacts to this words you are saying. Completely grasping this concept, you can start to see how you can surround yourself with positive energy. Me for one, I am attracted to people who are very optimistic, simply because they can shape their world with the thoughts in their hearts, and the words in their mouths. Something difficult will happen to people, and there will always be challenges to be faced, and mountains to be moved. Your reaction, however, is what determines your results, how you chose to see your situation. Think about this: do you always see your glass as half full, or half empty? If the former is how you see things, then good for you, but if the latter is how you see things, then you must do better. All of these things sound very difficult to do, but some uncomfortable things happen to make us, "us." There outcomes that seem to break us, so we can build ourselves up again. So here is what you do the next time you are faced with challenges, and you are tempted to look at the negative. Look for the positive thing in that situation even if it is only one thing, and focus on it. In fact, find opportunities from it. Other things that can help you to be more positive, is by effecting people in a positive way and the kind of relationships you have; the things you chose to invest your time in; doing something for someone-else; bring about dynamic exchange of the flow of giving-and-receiving in your life. I have learned that giving the very thing I need most reciprocated into more than enough, a companied by faith what you listen to and even the environment you live in mentally play a important role in the manifestation. So, you might want analyze what you let into your mind, and evaluate it carefully. You may need to eradicate the negativity to protect your space and your sanity; so, start by spending less time with those people who perpetuate negativity, and pump in some life-changing, mind-orienting, positive confessions into your life. This is also self-fulfilling, and it helps to keep you in sync with 'pure potential' from which all things arrive. Finally, thanks given is a very vital way to remain positive and defining a purpose that service others is the most fulfilling action one can do and bring unseen happiness onto you.

JOSHUA PENN, CNHP

Authors Notes

After losing my grandparents to cancer & becoming a practitioner I started to reflect and came to the understanding that we really have to do a better job with our overall health. We say things like, "I know this isn't good for me," or "We gonna die from something," and continue the toxic habits for no other reason than the pleasure of taste, or because were comfortable in the situation etc. Not realizing how selfish that is for those who care about us, when you pass way leaving behind broken hearts all because you were not willing to change, to become a better version of yourself. I personally found five ways to stay on track toward a greater me, while doing a job I was over-qualified for, and not interested in or happy. I thought about what I needed to do to, to feel that no matter how my day went, if I completed these things, I could always consider that day productive for what really important. Writing them down and reading them first thing in the morning and right before bed, manifested, what I had predicted into reality. Acting as a guide, I was able to focus with intention and get control over my life. We say we love our families and will do anything for them, well how about abandon all procrastination and gain a healthier balance with mind, body & spirit so that you can be around to enjoy them?! Not to mention enjoying yourself. Now I leave you with one question to ask yourself whether it's the food, spiritual or the mental aspect, are you the best version of you?

Made in the USA
Columbia, SC
23 March 2019